DRAWING PAD FOR KIDS